Foundations of Pre-Sales

A handbook and practical guide to a successful career as a solutions architect in pre-sales

Nathaniel F. Fagundo

Title: Foundations of Pre-Sales

Author: Nathaniel F. Fagundo

Self-Published

Copyright: 2023

First Edition, 2023

©

CONTENTS

PROLOGUE

    THE BEGINNING OF SOMETHING GREAT 5

CHAPTER 1

    INTRODUCTION TO PRE-SALES 8
    WHAT ARE PRE-SALES? 9
    BEING A TECHNICAL EVANGELIST 12
    THE CULTURE OF PRE-SALES 13
    QUALITIES FOR SUCCESS 13
    THE FUNDAMENTALS 17

CHAPTER 2

    THE POWER OF EFFECTIVE COMMUNICATION 20
    TWO EARS, ONE MOUTH 23
    TAILORING YOUR CONVERSATION TO YOUR AUDIENCE 25

CHAPTER 3

    TECHNICAL ACUMEN 29
    THE IMPORTANCE OF TECHNICAL MASTERY 31

CHAPTER 4

    SALES ACUMEN 34
    PRE-SALES VS. SALES 36
    FORECASTING 37

CHAPTER 5

    THE PRE-SALES PROCESS 39
    SOLUTION DESIGN, ANALYSIS, AND DELIVERY 40
    THE TECHNICAL WIN 42

CHAPTER 6

BUILDING STRONG CUSTOMER RELATIONSHIPS 45
ESTABLISHING TRUST 46
TRUSTED ADVISOR 48
BUILDING YOUR BRAND 50

CHAPTER 7

LEADERSHIP 55
LEADER OF PEOPLE 56
LEADERSHIP OF INDUSTRY 60
LEADERSHIP OF THE SALES TEAM 61
LEADERS OF LEADERS 62

CHAPTER 8

THE FUTURE OF PRE-SALES 67
CAREER ADVANCEMENT OPPORTUNITIES 69
PRODUCT MANAGEMENT 71
FIELD CTO 73
PRINCIPAL SOLUTIONS ARCHITECT 74
MANAGEMENT 75

CHAPTER 9

FINAL THOUGHTS 79
TO INFINITY AND… 81
CALL TO ACTION 85

ABOUT THE AUTHOR 90

Prologue

The Beginning of Something Great

Face front, true believers!

—Stan Lee

Welcome to the exciting world of pre-sales! As a pre-sales professional, you play a critical role in identifying and developing potential sales opportunities for your organization. Your ability to understand customer needs, propose solutions that meet those needs, and build trust and relationships with customers is crucial to your success in this field.

Whether you're new to this type of work or are already a seasoned professional, it's important to remember the fundamentals. In this book, we'll review several topics, from the skills needed to succeed to future potential career opportunities you can grow into.

Now, if you're new to pre-sales, I know it all can seem overwhelming at first. But as you read through this book, a lot of it will come easier than you think. I remember how overwhelming it was for me at the beginning of my career. The first time I joined a customer facing sales call I was so nervous I almost completely sweated through my shirt. One of the sales guys even thought I ran to the office that morning. But it's normal to feel nervous and overwhelmed in the beginning. That means you're diligent about doing a good job. Hold on to that passion and use it to power yourself through the early steps of your career.

It will feel like drinking through a firehose at first, but it gets better. After a while, you'll get comfortable with the role, then you'll really start enjoying it. You won't even realize it's happening until one day when you think back to where you were a year ago. Then you'll realize how much you've grown. When that happens, the concepts in this book will seem like common sense. Because, unbeknownst to you, you're no longer "new," but are becoming a true professional in the field.

Fundamentals naturally seem obvious to someone with years of experience.

At that point, you'll be working on more advanced skills to hone your craft, but it will all build off the basics. Even top professionals become busy and distracted. That's why everyone can use an occasional reminder of what's important in pre-sales. Before you get there, you must take the first steps in becoming a true pre-sales professional.

Regardless of whether you're in the early stages of your career or have gained extensive experience, it remains crucial to invest in personal development continuously. Reading this book is one of many investments you'll make throughout your professional journey. The contents offer valuable insights and knowledge that will empower you to progress further in your chosen path. This is just one example of your commitment to self-improvement and pursuing excellence in your career. This book serves to complement your existing efforts to expand your skills and capitalize on future opportunities.

Chapter 1

Introduction to Pre-Sales

You must expect great things of yourself before you can do them.

—*Michael Jordan*

Now let's get started by laying out some of the terms, titles, and qualities used in pre-sales. This chapter functions as a high-level introduction before we dive into some of these subjects in more depth later in the book. Let's first start by talking about what the responsibilities for a pre-sales professional are.

From a high level, pre-sales works with cross-functional teams in their field to identify customer needs and design solutions that meet those needs. This may include individuals from sales, engineering, services, product management, and other key stakeholders in their company. We create detailed proposals and presentations, as well as defend those proposals to potential customers.

The pre-sales process requires technical skills, business acumen, communication, and people-skills. You will need to stay up to date with the latest technologies and trends while working well with others. This will be critical to your success in this field.

Pre-Sales is constantly evolving, so continuous learning and development are essential. All while adapting to new technologies and trends and working well with others. The ability to evolve and think critically will be your key to achieving success.

What are Pre-Sales?

Pre-Sales is a term used to describe the work done before the actual sales process begins. This term includes activities such as market research, customer outreach, strategic planning, and product demonstrations.

The role of pre-sales in a sales campaign is to provide potential customers with the information and support they need to make an informed decision about purchasing a product or service. These expectations can include providing technical expertise, answering questions, and helping identify the best solutions for a customer's needs. By doing this, pre-sales professionals can help build trust and credibility with potential customers and set the stage for successful sales in the future. In the context of pre-sales, we sometimes refer to this as being a "Trusted Advisor."

Being a trusted advisor means being seen by customers as a reliable and knowledgeable source of guidance and support. To have customers trust you as a pre-sales advisor, we need to listen carefully to our customer's needs and concerns while providing honest advice and unbiased recommendations. We should demonstrate our technical expertise by offering insights and ideas that help the customer make informed decisions. We can only do this by understanding the customer's industry and business thoroughly.

Now there are several titles you could have under the pre-sales "umbrella." Though the titles may be different, many of the core responsibilities remain the same. Depending on the field you specialize in and your company's focus, there are a few titles. The most popular pre-sales titles are "solutions architect" and "systems engineer." Pre-Sales also uses titles like "technical consultant" and "sales engineer." The difference separating the roles is their technological focus and level of expertise. For the sake of simplicity, I will primarily use the term solutions architect for most of this book as a title for a pre-sales professional, as it's the most common and widely used title in the high-tech industry today.

A solutions architect is typically a high-level technical expert with a broad understanding of a wide range of technology solutions who can design and implement complex, enterprise-level systems. They're often involved in the early stages of the sales process and work closely with customers to gain a better understanding of their business needs and goals, to design customized solutions to meet those requirements.

A solutions architect is generally responsible for the big-picture design and overall strategy. A systems engineer, however, handles the technical details, implementation, and is typically a more specialized technical expert with deep expertise in a specific technology or area of focus. While they may be involved in the pre-sales process, they are more likely to join later to provide detailed technical support and guidance. Along with that, systems engineers need to ensure the proposed solution is feasible and can be implemented successfully.

Being a Technical Evangelist

One of the most outstanding titles anyone in the technology field can achieve is that of a technical evangelist. The reason is that it's an unofficial title given to someone by other individuals in their industry. Technical evangelists are typically experts in their field and deeply understand the technical details and capabilities of the products they promote. They're also skilled communicators and can explain complex technical concepts in a way that's easy for others to understand. It's not a title someone can give themselves. It belongs to a person passionate about a particular technology or product and who strives to educate and inspire others about its benefits and uses. Those are key roles in large technology companies, and their primary responsibility is to promote and explain the technical aspects of a product or service to potential customers and other stakeholders.

Besides promoting the technical aspects of a product or service, technical evangelists also play a crucial role in helping build enthusiasm and excitement around a technology or product. They often speak at conferences, meetups, and other events. They leverage their knowledge and passion to inspire others about the potential of the technology they're promoting. To get their message across effectively, technical evangelists must focus on building technical expertise, communication skills, and have a passion for their industry.

The Culture of Pre-Sales

The culture of pre-sales often focuses on collaboration and teamwork. Pre-Sales professionals work closely with sales, marketing teams, and other stakeholders to ensure customers have a positive experience throughout the sales cycle.

In many organizations, the pre-sales culture also focuses on innovation and continuous learning. Pre-Sales professionals must keep up to date with the latest products, technologies, and industry trends so they can share their knowledge and expertise with others.

The culture of pre-sales also involves a strong emphasis on customer service. Pre-Sales professionals must provide high-quality support and assistance to customers to help them make the best decision to meet their needs.

Overall, the pre-sales culture concentrates on a few key tenets, such as collaboration, innovation, continuous learning, and customer service. By fostering this culture, organizations can ensure their pre-sales teams can provide the best possible support to customers and drive success for the organization.

Qualities for Success

There are several qualities needed to achieve success in this industry. As I've previously stated, the most successful individuals have a combination of knowledge and soft skills. Soft skills are not taught and are the gifts that come naturally to an individual. Some examples of this would include how you interact with people, your demeanor, and ability to tell an engaging story. This allows them to boil complex technical solutions down into business-oriented outcomes effectively for their customers. Doing that requires practical communication skills, technical expertise, sales acumen, and trustworthiness.

Effective communication is essential in pre-sales. It includes the ability to convey information clearly and concisely to potential customers all while listening and responding to their questions and concerns. Two significant components of effective communication are knowing who you're speaking with and how you choose to get your message across to them. A few popular examples of these communication methods include using a whiteboard, PowerPoint, storytelling, etc.

It's essential to understand what your strengths and weaknesses are so you can more effectively get your message across. It's vital to know your audience so you can keep your messaging relevant to them. For example, you may talk about "Speeds and Feeds" to a system administrator with hands-on experience with the technology, but a C-level executive couldn't care less about the technical details. C-level executives play a strategic role within an organization and focus on making decisions that better the entire company. Depending on the executive, they're typically in charge of an entire department or business unit, such as marketing, finance, operations, or IT.

Another important skill for any pre-sales professional is having strong technical expertise. A deep understanding of the products and services being sold is critical. It's just as essential to have the ability to understand the needs and challenges of potential customers. Not only must you understand your technical solutions, you also need to know how those solutions fit into a customer's environment. Then you need to recognize how those pieces support the customer's business. After that, you can start mapping how your technology can create value for your customer's business.

Along with technical expertise, pre-sales professionals must also have strong sales skills; after all, "sales" is in the name. There's a lot of good advice out in the world explaining what you need to be a successful salesperson, and a lot of that also applies to an individual in pre-sales. Some examples include the ability to identify potential customers, understand their needs, and communicate the value of a product or service effectively so it resonates with those customers. But the fundamental goal of a pre-sales engineer/architect differs from that of their sales counterparts. A sales representative's goal is to ultimately meet their quota, whereas the solutions architect's primary goal is to achieve the "Technical Win." This means the customer believes you have the best technology for their business regardless of price. We'll explore the technical win in a later chapter, but achieving this means you've done everything possible to give sales the best chance of success.

The most challenging thing to earn, while being the easiest to lose, is trust. Trust is a critical component of the customer-vendor relationship. Customers rely on pre-sales to provide them with honest, unbiased advice and recommendations while acting in their best interests.

Start building trust by actively listening to customers and showing a genuine interest in understanding their unique requirements. You should also provide honest information about products or services, especially including what their capabilities and limitations are. You want to make sure to always under promise and over deliver to set the customer up for a positive experience. Pre-sales professionals can showcase their expertise through case studies, testimonials, or references from satisfied customers. Building long-term relationships by consistently delivering on promises, providing excellent customer service, and responding to customer inquiries further strengthens trust.

Suppose customers don't see a solutions architect as trustworthy. That would damage their credibility and reputation, making it difficult to build long-term customer relationships. It would also make it difficult for the sales team to feel they can rely on their solutions architect. Reliability helps build trust and confidence among team members, leading to increased collaboration and more effective problem-solving.

Overall, trustworthiness is an essential quality for any pre-sales solutions architect, as it helps ensure that they can effectively serve their customers and contribute to the success of their organization.

The Fundamentals

We can measure success in pre-sales in various ways, depending on the individual and the organization they work for. Success involves meeting or exceeding sales targets, building solid customer relationships, providing valuable insights and feedback, and demonstrating technical and sales expertise. Let's touch on these in some more detail:

- **Meeting or exceeding sales targets.** This is often one of the primary measures of success in sales. Sales teams and leadership highly value pre-sales professionals who consistently meet or exceed their sales targets. It shows a strong sales acumen, which we'll cover in later chapters.

- **Building solid customer relationships.** This involves building strong, long-lasting relationships with customers. Pre-Sales professionals who can establish trust and credibility will have a higher likely hood of a successful sales campaign as they offer the support customers need to make an informed decision. There's an old saying that says people buy from people they like. Those words remain relevant today.
- **Providing valuable insights and feedback.** Pre-Sales professionals must provide valuable insights and input for a customer's business from your interactions with customers and learning about their businesses. This can include identifying trends and patterns in customer behavior and providing suggestions for improving products and services.
- **Demonstrating technical and sales expertise.** To be successful in pre-sales, you must put talk into action. Sometimes this means thinking on your feet during a technical discussion to handle objections or jumping into a product demo last minute. It takes a combination of technical expertise and sales acumen to take a

complex technical solution and translate it into business outcomes.

These fundamentals are what make pre-sales so valuable to companies. You can help your organization grow by building trust and credibility with potential customers and setting the stage for successful sales. This requires combining technical expertise, sales acumen, and strong communication skills. We'll review these details in future chapters, starting with effective communication.

Chapter 2

The Power of Effective Communication

Good communication is just as stimulating as black coffee, and just as hard to sleep after.

—*Anne Morrow Lindbergh*

Effective communication is one of the essential skills you must possess as a solutions architect. Effective communication is the process of exchanging information and ideas in a clear, concise way that is easily understood by others. This involves using a variety of mediums, such as speaking, writing, and nonverbal cues, to convey information and ideas accurately and efficiently. It doesn't matter how technical and trustworthy you are if you can't convey your message to your audience. There are many ways to communicate effectively, depending on the situation and the audience. Some examples of different ways to communicate effectively include:

- **Speaking.** Now this may seem obvious, but there's more to speaking than the words that come out of your mouth. It also includes the environment you're speaking in. For example: face-to-face meetings, presentations, and public speaking. To communicate effectively through speaking, use clear and concise language and speak at a pace that's easy for others to follow. You should also use nonverbal cues, such as body language and eye contact, to support your message.
- **Writing.** Another effective way to communicate is through writing. This includes emails, reports, and other written materials. To communicate effectively through writing, use clear, concise language and organize your thoughts in a logical, easy-to-follow manner. You should also proofread your writing to ensure it's free of errors and typos.
- **Visual aids.** Visual aids, such as graphs, charts, and images, can be a powerful tool for effective communication. They can help clarify complex concepts

and ideas and make information easier to understand and remember. I'm sure you've heard the adage, "A picture is worth a thousand words." To use visual aids effectively, choose relevant and visually appealing materials to supplement, rather than replace, verbal communication.

These categories of communication are nothing new, but they're an essential foundation you must master to be an effective communicator. After mastering these basic methods, you can combine them into more advanced communication methods, like with a whiteboard or product demo. These are used to communicate ideas, concepts, and solutions more easily to customers, team members, and other stakeholders. Whiteboarding and product demos provide a visual and interactive way to explain complex ideas and concepts and can help to engage and persuade others.

For pre-sales professionals, whiteboarding and product demos are critical because they often demonstrate a product's or solution's value and capabilities to potential customers. Allowing you to more effectively communicate the benefits of a product or solution and help persuade customers to adopt new technology.

In addition, whiteboarding and product demos can also be helpful for internal communication and problem-solving. They can help clarify and solidify ideas, providing a visual to facilitate collaboration and discussion among team members. These are also popular methods favored by pre-sales professionals since they allow people to visualize a concept or idea.

Overall, being effective at different forms of communication is an essential skill, serving to effectively explain a product's value and improving internal collaboration within your organization. Making this an invaluable asset in both external sales efforts and internal team dynamics.

Two Ears, One Mouth

Effective communication is a two-way street. It involves actively listening to others and responding to their questions and concerns. That means paying attention to what others say, asking clarifying questions, and providing feedback and support when needed. This keeps the conversation engaging and relevant to the customer's interests and goals. For example, have you ever had a friend where your conversations always seem to revolve around them and their interests? Ever notice how they're usually the ones doing all the talking? That's a perfect example of what you want to avoid. A good rule of thumb is to follow the "80/20 rule."

The 80/20 rule for active listening suggests that effective listeners should spend 80% of their time listening and 20% speaking. That means you should focus on understanding and absorbing what the other person is saying rather than simply waiting for your turn to speak. By following the 80/20 rule, you can show the speaker that you're genuinely interested in what they have to say. Then you're more likely to understand their perspectives and needs.

To follow the 80/20 rule for active listening, practice maintaining eye contact, asking clarifying questions, and paraphrasing what the speaker said to ensure you have understood correctly. You should also avoid interrupting the speaker and allow them to fully express their thoughts and feelings before responding. Don't listen just to reply, listen to understand. When you do speak, make sure it is thoughtful and helps spur the conversation deeper. By following the 80/20 rule and actively listening to others, you can build stronger relationships with customers and team members to be a more effective communicator and problem-solver.

Tailoring Your Conversation to Your Audience

Effective communication also involves adapting to the audience's needs and preferences. That means tailoring the content and delivery of a message to that specific audience, using jargon and examples relatable to them. It's essential to tailor your conversation to your audience because doing so helps ensure that the people you're communicating with understood and received your message effectively.

When you tailor your conversation to your audience, you can present information in a relevant and meaningful way to them, which makes it more likely that they will listen, engage, and remember what you have to say. For example, you may review the technical details of a solution with a system admin, since they'll interact with the technology daily. If you speak to a C-level executive, however, you'll want to keep your talk track at a higher level by focusing on the solution's business outcomes.

There are several critical benefits to tailoring your conversation to your audience. First, it helps build rapport and establish trust. When you speak in a way that is tailored to your audience, you show you understand and respect their needs, concerns, and interests, which can help to build trust and establish a more productive relationship.

Second, when you present information to your audience in a relevant and meaningful way, they're more likely to pay attention, ask questions, and take part in the conversation. That leads to more constructive discussions, which facilitate better decision-making and problem-solving. The best conversations have enthusiastic engagement and participation from everyone.

Finally, molding your conversation to your listeners will increase the effectiveness of getting your message across to them. Be aware of the terms and communication methods specific to each audience. For example, if you're speaking to a CIO, focus on business-centric terms like ROI, TCO, revenue growth, and strategic alignment. Conversely when speaking to a system administrator, emphasize the technical details, configuration options, compatibility support, security benefits, and troubleshooting enhancements. Adapting your language and approach to the specific needs and responsibilities of each role enhances understanding and facilitates effective communication. This may sound obvious, but it's surprisingly uncommon. Most people speak to everyone in the same manner, which is much less effective.

As a pre-sales solutions architect, you must tailor your talk track to a variety of customers. For example, in IT, customers include roles like:

- **IT managers.** IT managers will have different needs and concerns depending on the organization's size. The vast majority may focus on cost-effectiveness, simplicity, and risk mitigation. Be sure they understand the value and benefits of your solutions in a relevant and meaningful way to them.
- **IT professionals.** IT professionals, such as network or systems administrators, may be more interested in technical details and capabilities. They need to understand how your solutions integrate into their existing systems and processes. It's essential to explain the technical aspects of your solutions and address any concerns they may have.
- **Executives.** Executives, such as CEOs or CTOs, focus more on strategic goals and long-term planning. Therefore, they may be less interested in the technical details. It's crucial to ensure you can effectively communicate your solution's business value and strategic benefits for their goals, to earn their support.
- **Decision-makers/Gatekeepers.** Decision-makers and Gatekeepers are usually the ones responsible for evaluating and approving your solutions. Some examples of these would be department heads or purchasing managers. Their primary focus is to look out

for the best interests of their department. Usually, their decisions are based on price, ROI, and value.

Overall, as a pre-sales solutions architects you must tailor your conversation to the individual you're speaking to because doing so helps to ensure customers understand your message and the value of the solutions you provide. Otherwise, you will fail to build rapport, engage your audience, and achieve the desired outcomes of your conversation with your customers.

There are many ways to communicate effectively, and the best approach depends on the situation and the audience. Being an effective communicator will build strong relationships through conveying information and ideas to providing people with an understanding of complex concepts and ideas. To me, more succinctly, it allows you to provide value.

Chapter 3

Technical Acumen

Technical skill is mastery of complexity, while creativity is mastery of simplicity.

—*Christopher Zeeman*

Technical acumen refers to a person's knowledge and expertise in a particular technical field or subject. This is a foundational requirement for all pre-sales professionals since organizations consider this role to be a technical one. You can develop technical acumen in several ways, such as through individual studies, formalized training, and professional experiences. We typically acquire technical acumen through experience in roles requiring high-level technical knowledge and expertise. For example, a software engineer might have high levels of technical acumen in programming languages, algorithms, and data structures. A medical doctor has a thorough understanding of anatomy, physiology, and medical treatments.

A great technical understanding is essential. It allows you to understand complex technical concepts and apply that knowledge to real-world problems. Technical acumen can also help you communicate effectively with experts in your field. There are many ways you can improve your technical knowledge. Some ways you can do this include:

- Taking courses or attending workshops to learn new technical skills or to deepen your understanding of existing ones.
- Reading technical books or articles to stay up to date with the latest developments in your field.
- Participating in online forums or discussion groups to connect with other professionals and learn from their experiences.
- Attending conferences or industry events to network with others and learn about new technologies and techniques.

- Practicing and applying the skills you learn through real-world projects, hands-on exercises, and simulations.
- Staying up to date with industry trends and developments, including new technologies, market shifts, and changing customer needs and expectations.
- Gaining hands-on experience and seeking opportunities to work on real-world projects and challenges and get hands-on experience with new technologies and tools.
- Seeking guidance and mentorship from more experienced professionals, including working with a mentor, joining a professional organization, or participating in professional development programs.

The Importance of Technical Mastery

As shown in the previous section, it's essential to be technical as a solutions architect. This is because you're responsible for designing and implementing complex technology solutions for your customers. To do this effectively, solutions architects need to have a deep understanding of a wide range of technologies while possessing the ability to analyze and acknowledge complex business requirements and your goals. Having robust technical knowledge is a vital requirement for the job.

It helps if a solutions architect has a genuine interest in technology. Enthusiasm and a genuine interest in your field drives continuous learning and exploration. It will enable you to keep pace with fast-moving industry trends and best practices. A passion for technology empowers solutions architects to absorb new technology and adapt effectively. Moreover, it helps prevent burnout by providing intrinsic motivation and a sense of fulfillment. It fuels our drive to overcome challenges, maintain engagement, and find joy in our work. Passion inspires creativity and innovation, allowing you to get creative and find novel solutions to complex problems.

Being very technical allows you to design cost-effective, scalable solutions and meet customers' unique needs. It also enables you to provide ongoing support and guidance to customers, helping them get the most out of their technology solutions over the long term.

In addition, your knowledge base is essential to build credibility and trust with customers and stakeholders. Customers want to know they're working with a knowledgeable and capable professional. Being technical allows you to show you're capable so that customers can trust you to be successful. It also helps build confidence and trust within the organization, as you'll provide valuable technical expertise and guidance to other team members.

Without a deep understanding of various technologies and the ability to analyze and understand business requirements, you may struggle to recommend and implement cost-effective, scalable solutions and meet the unique needs of your customers, which would quickly cause you to lose credibility with your sales team and customers.

If you aren't technical, you'll have difficulty providing technical support and expertise to potential customers, leaving customers needing more information and assistance to make an informed decision. Likely resulting in the sale falling through. We will talk more about ways you can improve your technical knowledge in later chapters.

Chapter 4

Sales Acumen

Approach each customer with the idea of helping him or her solve a problem or achieve a goal, not of selling a product or service.

— Brian Tracy

Though the role of a solutions architect falls under the umbrella of "sales," you aren't a sales representative. It's essential to draw a line between the difference in the two roles of "pre-sales" and "sales." A solutions architect isn't the same thing as a sales representative, though they work together. That means understanding each other's roles and responsibilities is crucial. As previously stated, you'll be more successful if you develop a strong sales acumen to support your technical acumen.

Sales acumen refers to a person's understanding and knowledge of the principles and practices of sales. For someone working in pre-sales, sales acumen is the ability to understand and communicate the value and benefits of a product or solution to potential customers effectively. This involves the art of persuading them to make a purchase or adopt a decision. This doesn't mean trying to "sell someone," but rather to communicate the value of your solution effectively to address a customer's needs and concerns.

Pre-Sales professionals are also often responsible for identifying potential sales opportunities, so having a deep understanding of sales techniques and strategies is essential for your success in this role. It also involves understanding market trends and dynamics, in order to adapt to changing customer needs and preferences. That requires negotiating effectively, closing deals, and building long-term customer relationships.

Now, there are thousands of books on sales, so we won't go in-depth there. However, it's still crucial to understand the role and how it relates to pre-sales. If you know what drives an individual, then you know how to better work with them to form an effective team.

Pre-Sales vs. Sales

Each role's focus is necessary for a successful sales team, but how they go about it is unique to each position. How sales and pre-sales folks look at things fundamentally differs. This affects everything from how they look at sales opportunities to how they work with customers. Everyone has a role in supporting their customers and their organization's requests.

There are many things that motivate sales representatives. One of the core motivations is the opportunity to earn financial rewards, such as commissions or bonuses. Conversely, solutions architects simply are inspired when working on complex and intellectually challenging problems. Primarily, the opportunity to design and implement innovative technology solutions motivates them.

As a solutions architect, you'll leverage your technical expertise and knowledge to provide detailed explanations of the solution details. You can then correlate the technical differentiations by addressing the customer's needs directly. Sales representatives, however, may focus more on the results and value of the solutions, rather than on the details of how they achieved that outcome.

Since solutions architects go deep into technical discussions with customers to understand their specific needs and requirements, it can be a very time-consuming process. Still, the time spent doing this is necessary if you want to be thorough. Sales representatives are more focused on progressing the sales opportunity by keeping things organized and on-track. They are far more time sensitive since they're primarily responsible for sales forecasting and meeting the customers' required timelines.

After the sale, solutions architects may offer ongoing support and guidance to customers, helping them get the most from their purchased solutions. Sometimes, they even assist with integrating the new technology into a customer's environment. If the customer has any issues, the solutions architect will typically jump in to get the resources needed to help. In some rare cases, they may go as far as troubleshooting the issues themselves. On the other hand, sales representatives are traditionally more focused on maintaining customer relationships, but cannot offer much help post-sale, aside from looping in specific technical resources when needed.

Forecasting

Now, let's touch upon the least enjoyable piece of sales; forecasting. Sales representatives forecast sales by predicting when deals will close and for how much. Every sales organization has their own style for how they forecast, but everyone does it in some form. Whether it's indicating opportunities by a percentage or with a "gut feel," all sales professionals must forecast their numbers for their organization. For example, some sales organizations use percentages like 30%, 60%, 90%, etc., to show how their opportunities progress toward closing. Other organizations may use terms like "upside," "high upside," and "commit" to describe a "gut feeling" about how far along an opportunity may be. Regardless of the measurement used to forecast, the end goal is the same. To track a sales opportunity from cradle to the grave.

Pre-Sales folks track sales opportunities as well, but it's a little different from sales. We aren't as worried about the deal closing as much as we are about tracking our responsibility for the sales campaign. A solutions architect may track a sales opportunity through different phases, such as discovery, analysis, design, and defense. This helps ensure the proposed solution meets the customer's needs and addresses any challenges or risks. This is all part of the pre-sales process which we'll review in greater in the next chapter.

Chapter 5

The Pre-Sales Process

If I had an hour to solve a problem, I'd spend 55 minutes thinking about the problem and 5 minutes thinking about solutions.

— *Albert Einstein*

The pre-sales process is based on consultative selling that emphasizes understanding the customer's needs, challenges, and goals to propose solutions that address those needs. This way of consultative selling differs from traditional selling as it focuses on understanding the customer's needs and providing solutions that directly meet those needs rather than simply pushing a product or service. The process typically involves four stages: Discover, Analyze, Design, and Defend. It's very similar to the scientific method you may have learned about in school. The scientific method is a logical problem-solving approach used by scientists to answer questions about the natural world. It involves several steps, including making observations, asking questions, forming a hypothesis, making a prediction based on the hypothesis, testing the prediction, and iterating by using the results to make new hypotheses or predictions.

When you think about it, it's almost exactly like the pre-sales process. Both involve making observations (discovery), asking questions (analyze), forming hypotheses (design), and testing predictions (defend). However, the pre-sales process focuses on understanding and meeting the customer's needs with a company's goods or services, while the scientific method is used to answer questions about the natural world. Now we'll review the steps of the pre-sales process.

Solution Design, Analysis, and Delivery

The first step is research. During this discovery phase, as a solutions architect, you will work alongside the sales team to identify and understand the customer's needs and requirements. This may involve gathering information about the customer's business, technology environment, and goals, as well as conducting interviews or workshops with key stakeholders. That way, you can gain a wholistic understanding of the customer's environment. This data-gathering phase is one of the most important stages because it's the basis for the rest of the process. More data in leads to better data out.

In the analysis phase, you sort and review the information gathered during the discovery phase to develop a solution to meet the customer's needs. This involves evaluating different options, assessing the feasibility and cost of different approaches, and identifying potential challenges or risks. Taking your time here is essential to ensure you miss nothing and consider every possible option. This is where being an "outside the box" kind of thinker comes in handy. Looking at a problem from different perspectives shows you possess a good understanding of the customer's needs and allows you to architect a solution that will differentiate your offering from your competitors.

All the preparation until now reminds me of what a chef would call *mise en place*. *Mise en place* is a French term that means "putting in place" and refers to preparing and organizing all ingredients, equipment, and tools needed to execute a recipe or technique.

Now comes the design phase, where the rubber meets the road. That's when you, as a solutions architect, work to design a detailed solution that meets the customer's needs. That may involve creating intricate technical designs, developing implementation plans, and identifying resources or support needed to implement the solution. You might use a combination of sizing tools, Visio, PowerPoint, etc., to create a proposal for the customer. The design phase should be simple if the discovery and analysis phases are correctly done.

Finally, you need to defend all the work you've done until this point. This phase is where you can finally share the details of your solution, show your research, field questions, and defend your work. This is "Game Day" for a solutions architect and is your chance to present and defend your proposed solution to the customer. It may involve conducting a presentation with demonstrations, answering questions, and addressing any concerns the customer may have. If done successfully, it's at this stage solutions architects can achieve the "Technical Win."

The Technical Win

Two words, technical win, define success for a pre-sales solutions architect in a sales campaign. Achieving a technical win, or a tech win, in a sales campaign means successfully persuading a customer to adopt a technology solution based on its technical capabilities and features, regardless of price.

Achieving a tech win can be especially important in sales campaigns where the solution's technical capabilities are a crucial differentiator, or the customer has specific technical requirements you must fulfill to close the sale. By demonstrating the technical value of the solution and addressing technical concerns, the sales team can build credibility with the customer and increase the chances of closing the deal.

Achieving a tech win isn't the same as closing the sale, as there may be other factors the customer considers when making a purchase decision. However, it's an essential step in the sales process and will increase the chances of closing the deal.

There are several ways you can know, as a solutions architect, if you have the tech win in a sales campaign. One of the simplest and most reliable ways to know is to ask the customer for feedback on the technical aspects of the solution. That might involve asking specific questions about the solution's capabilities and features and how they compare to the competition.

Another way to know if you have the tech win is to pay attention to the technical questions the customer asks. If they ask in-depth technical questions about the solution, they may be interested in and impressed by its technical capabilities. Suppose the customer raises technical objections or concerns during the sales process. In that case, that may signify they're considering the technical aspects of the solution and are weighing the pros and cons. You can increase the chances of achieving the tech win by effectively addressing these objections.

The hope is, at this stage, the customer expresses a solid commitment to adopting the solution based on its technical capabilities and features. In that case, it would be a clear sign that you have achieved the tech win. This may involve the customer indicating they're ready to purchase or expressing enthusiasm for the solution's technical capabilities.

Chapter 6

Building Strong Customer Relationships

Get closer than ever to your customers. So close that you tell them what they need well before they realize it themselves.

—Steve Jobs

A strong relationship with customers means a high level of trust, understanding, and communication between the customer and the business.

From the customer's perspective, a strong relationship means they feel respected and that your business responds to their concerns. They're more likely to be satisfied with their experience, recommend your products to others, and stay loyal to the business. They know they can rely on your company to provide quality offerings and that you're a leader in your area of expertise.

From the perspective of a pre-sales solutions architect, a strong relationship with customers means you have a deep understanding of the customer's business needs and can provide the right solutions to meet those needs. You must have a good account of the customer's business to anticipate their future needs by having regular interactions with them. Creating a strong relationship with the customer's decision-makers and influencers will earn their buy-in on future proposed solutions for their company. In essence, build customer trust by providing valuable insights and responding to their needs.

Having a solid relationship with customers benefits both the customer and your business. A positive customer experience results in repeat business and positive word-of-mouth recommendations. That's why it is crucial to build trust.

Establishing Trust

The most crucial tenet for anyone in pre-sales is "Trust." Instilling confidence is essential to building a solid foundation for relationships with customers and your sales team. Trust is a feeling of confidence in the reliability, truth, ability, or strength of someone. You build trust over time through consistent, reliable, and honest behavior. When someone consistently does what they say they'll do and acts with integrity, people are more likely to trust them.

You also build trust through transparency and open communication. When individuals are open and honest about their thoughts, feelings, and actions, others are more likely to trust them.

Having a customer's confidence is necessary for building solid and long-lasting relationships. We build customer confidence through consistent delivery of quality products or services, meeting commitments, and providing exceptional customer experiences. When customers trust someone or something, they're more likely to be loyal and to continue doing business with them.

A customer's trust is essential in many contexts, as it can influence their behavior and decisions. For example, a customer who trusts a particular brand is more likely to buy its products and recommend them to others. Customers who trust a specific service provider are more likely to use their services and provide positive feedback and referrals.

Trust and integrity are essential in pre-sales because they're both critical to the success of the sales process. Pre-Sales professionals play a crucial role in providing technical support and expertise to potential customers. That is a critical part of building a good relationship with your customers. Over time, your customers may even consider you a "trusted advisor."

Trusted Advisor

Let's talk about what a trusted advisor is and why it's a brand or quality to be treasured. A trusted advisor is someone people trust to act in their best interest and who has fully earned their confidence. Customers view that individual as a reliable source of information and guidance. This is something every pre-sales professional should strive to achieve one day.

Achieving this status as a trusted advisor isn't a onetime event, but a process that takes time and consistent effort to build. It requires effort to maintain, since trust is easily lost. It results from creating a positive and long-lasting relationship with the customer. There are a few shared areas that set a trusted advisor apart from their peers. Some of these attributes include:

- **Expertise.** Being knowledgeable in your field, while providing valuable insights and information that can help customers or clients achieve their goals.

- **Communication.** Being responsive and transparent in your communication by actively listening to provide quality feedback.
- **Integrity.** Acting honestly and always putting the customer's best interests first.
- **Consistency.** Providing consistent and reliable service and following through on commitments.
- **Personalization.** Customizing solutions and services to meet the specific needs of clients.
- **Responsiveness.** Being available and responsive, especially when people need you the most.
- **Empathy.** Showing understanding for your customer's own needs and concerns.
- **Proactivity.** Anticipating potential needs and providing a solution before being asked.

As a trusted advisor, customers and clients will turn to you for advice and guidance on important decisions. Essentially, you are part of their team. They have confidence in your expertise and professionalism, relying on you to act in their best interests. You should value that responsibility and take it seriously.

These qualities feed into people's perspectives of you as a professional. Regardless of your feelings, the world's perception of you is the reality. Another name for this is your "brand." Your brand is an intentional and conscious effort to influence the outward perception of yourself in the world. This is a crucial concept to be self-aware of since it directly impacts your future professional opportunities.

Building Your Brand

An individual can easily overlook the idea of their brand, but it's imperative in a field that relies on relationships and trust. Your brand is your reputation and how others perceive you in your professional network. Your brand includes your values, skills, expertise, and the unique value you bring to your work. A solid personal brand can help you stand out in your industry and can be a critical factor for a long, successful career.

Building a solid brand can help you differentiate yourself from others in your field and stand out in a crowded job market. When you have a well-defined brand, people are more likely to see you as an expert in your field and characterize you as a reputable resource. By highlighting your unique skills and expertise, you can make yourself more attractive to potential employers and clients to increase your visibility in your industry.

Building your brand is an ongoing process, but it's well worth the effort as it's a massive help in achieving your long-term career goals. By consistently presenting yourself as a knowledgeable and skilled professional, you can position yourself for success and increase your chances of advancing your career. Here are a few ways you can share your technical mastery while contributing to building your brand:

- **Earn relevant certifications.** Earning relevant certificates can demonstrate mastery of a specific technical topic effectively, as it shows you have achieved a certain level of knowledge and skills in a particular area of expertise.
- **Participate in technical communities.** Participating in technical communities, such as online forums or user groups, can help you share your knowledge and experience with others by contributing to technical discussions and problem-solving efforts.
- **Write technical articles or blog posts.** Writing technical articles or blog posts can effectively share your knowledge and expertise with a broader audience. It also records what you know so people can reference it in the future.
- **Present at technical conferences or events.** Giving presentations at technical meetings or events allows you to share your knowledge with a larger audience and engage with other professionals in your field.

- **Lead technical projects.** Leading technical projects show that you can take the lead on complex technical projects and successfully guide them to completion.
- **Create technical demonstrations.** Creating technical demonstrations, such as video tutorials or live demonstrations, can also be an excellent way to show hands-on expertise in technology. It can also help educate others in your field with a real-world application of what you've learned.
- **Contribute to open-source projects.** Contributing to open-source projects shows your ability to work with others to solve complex technical problems. By contributing to open-source projects, you can show your skills in a particular area and build your reputation and visibility in that technical community.
- **Teach or mentor others.** Teaching or mentoring others is a great way to give back to the same community that likely helped you in the early stages of your career. It can help the next generation of technical professionals and helps build your reputation as a thought leader.

An exercise you can do to stay focused on building the brand you want is to create a personal brand statement. A brand statement is one to three sentences explaining what you do and why you're unique in your field. It can touch on your experience, skills, and passions. It should be short but contain enough compelling information to convey your value and show your personality. If anyone saw it, they should easily understand who you are and what you offer. More importantly, they should agree that it accurately interprets who you are.

Unlike big muscles, you can't look at someone and know if they have a big brain. There are no visible signs for someone with extensive knowledge. So, the question becomes, how can you share your experiences and what you've learned over time? Having some technical expertise comes in handy for customer conversations, but that's not all it's useful for. It's essential to share what you know as part of building your brand. That's where I see many people with a ton of potential fall short and miss a golden opportunity.

A powerful brand can help you and others in your field in several ways. It will help you build credibility and trust with colleagues, customers, and other stakeholders. When you have a well-defined brand, people are more likely to see you as an expert in your field and trust your judgment. That can be especially important when working with customers, as it helps build loyalty and drive sales. It will also allow you to differentiate yourself from others in your field and stand out in a crowded job market.

By highlighting your unique skills and expertise, you can make yourself more attractive to potential employers and clients and increase your visibility in your industry. Not to mention, having a solid brand can enhance your reputation within your field and help others see you as a thought leader or subject matter expert. This can be especially valuable if you're looking to advance your career, as it can help position you for success and increase your opportunities for growth and advancement.

Overall, having a solid brand can benefit you and others in your field. It provides credibility, differentiates you from your peers, enhances your reputation, and provides you with influence. Thus, opening new doors of opportunities for you in your career. Allowing you to try new things and continue to progress your career. A notable example of one of these potential opportunities is leadership opportunities. Leadership is a term used frequently in pre-sales but has a different purpose depending on its context. Because of this, it's an important topic worthy of having a chapter of its own.

Chapter 7

Leadership

A leader knows the way, goes the way, and shows the way.

—*John Maxwell*

Leadership is a quality often overlooked, but it's an integral part of being in pre-sales. There are many ways someone can "be a leader." There are leaders of people, leaders in an industry, and leaders within your organization. Each of these forms of leadership comes with its own set of responsibilities and focuses. Leadership is essential as your career advances, and it takes time to learn to lead effectively. Let's peel back the onion and touch on each one of these forms of leadership and how they relate to pre-sales.

Leader of People

A people's leader is someone who leads and manages a team of individuals. They set goals, create a vision for the team, and provide guidance and support to team members. They focus on fostering a positive team culture, resolving conflicts, and providing mentorship and coaching.

Becoming a people's leader involves developing skills and behaviors that enable you to manage a team of individuals effectively. People's leaders typically focus on a few key areas that differ from what an individual contributor would.

- **Setting goals.** People's leaders set clear, measurable goals for their team and ensure that team members understand how their work fits into the organization's overall objectives.
- **Providing guidance.** People's leaders offer guidance and support to team members, helping them navigate challenges and overcome obstacles.
- **Building a positive team culture.** People's leaders foster a positive and inclusive team culture that promotes collaboration and teamwork.

- **Developing team members.** People's leaders invest in developing their team members by providing opportunities for professional growth and encouraging continuous improvement.
- **Communicating effectively.** People's leaders must communicate effectively with team members, providing clear direction, feedback, and support.
- **Managing conflicts.** People's leaders must manage conflicts effectively and help team members constructively resolve differences.
- **Making decisions.** People's leaders must be able to make decisions in the best interest of the team and the organization.
- **Empowering.** People's leaders must empower their team members to make decisions and take ownership of their work.
- **Lead by example.** People's leaders must lead by example, demonstrating the behaviors and attitudes they expect from their team members.
- **Flexibility.** People's leaders must be flexible and adaptable in their leadership style and can adjust to the needs of their team members and the organization.

Now, if becoming a people's leader is something you're passionate about, you may want to pursue a career in management. If so, there are a few things you can do to prepare for when an opportunity to step into management presents itself.

There are some fundamental things you can work toward to help stack the deck in your favor if you want to pursue a management role in pre-sales. The simplest way to prepare is by looking at what your existing leadership is doing, then volunteer to help with those activities. It sounds elementary, but sometimes the most straightforward solutions are the most effective. Take on additional responsibilities that demonstrate your ability to manage projects and people effectively. This will allow you to show you have leadership skills and have developed the experience to handle the challenges of a management role.

As we discussed, your network and personal brand is also essential as it allows you to build relationships with key stakeholders that could impact your applications for a management role. That includes your customers, colleagues, and senior management. You'll need to gain their support and trust, which is necessary for success in a management role. Seek additional professional development opportunities, such as attending conferences, workshops, or simply taking on additional responsibilities within your team. It's imperative to have laid the groundwork to prepare for a management opportunity in advance of an actual position being open. This will help you develop the skills and knowledge essential for success in a management role.

As you prepare for a step into management, you'll need the skills for the job before opportunities arise. Many people think you need luck to move into management, but luck is just when your preparation meets the right opportunity. Create your own luck by being prepared and taking advantage of all the opportunities to be a leader as they come your way.

While working in management comes with its fair share of challenges, it provides a unique opportunity to make a positive impact on people's lives. As a manager, you have the power to enhance the well-being and success of your team members. By providing support, encouragement, and opportunities for growth, you can help individuals develop their skills, achieve their goals, and unlock their full potential. You can also create a supportive and inclusive work environment that promotes work-life balance, professional fulfillment, and personal satisfaction. By recognizing and nurturing your team's strengths and talents, you can truly make a difference and contribute to making their lives better.

In short, being a people's leader creates an environment where team members feel motivated, supported, and engaged in their work. It also involves fostering a positive culture, providing guidance, and investing in the development of team members. You must communicate effectively, manage conflicts, make decisions, and lead by example. It's a demanding role, but it can be very rewarding for individuals who enjoy helping others succeed.

Leadership of Industry

Being a leader in your industry and being a people's leader involves different skills and responsibilities. The common term for this is a "thought leader." A thought leader is traditionally someone considered an authority by their peers in their field of concentration.

A pre-sales professional, who is also a thought leader, significantly contributes to their industry. Your primary focus as a thought leader is on being recognized as an expert in your field. This means staying current on industry trends, best practices, and modern technologies. Other professionals will likely come to you for your advice and insights in your field.

Not only is it essential for thought leaders to stay informed about the latest industry trends and best practices, but it's also equally important that you share your knowledge and insights as well. Knowledge can be gained through reading industry publications, attending conferences, and networking with peers.

But then you can share that knowledge with others by writing articles, giving presentations, or taking part in other groups in the industry. It's important to network with other industry professionals and build relationships to establish yourself as a valuable resource. Being a thought leader in an industry is about staying current with the trends.

A people's leader's primary focus is on managing and leading a team of individuals and creating an environment where team members feel motivated, supported, and engaged in their work. A thought leader focuses on their involvement in their field of work. Each attribute has its own values, but equal importance, in being a powerful leader.

Leadership of the Sales Team

Being a leader on a sales team shares a lot of similarities to the other leadership types, but with its own twist. All three roles have similar responsibilities like setting goals, providing guidance, making decisions, and leading by example. However, their focus is fundamentally different. A sales team leader's primary focus is on the sales organizations success and on achieving the company's sales goals. That may include developing sales targets, creating a sales strategy, and providing guidance to team members, as the sales team's success reflects your success.

Being a sales team leader also means ensuring the team is productive, motivated, and aligned with the company's goals. This means thinking on your feet to overcome any challenges that may suddenly arise. You must also be able to identify and address any issues or challenges that may arise within the team. Then you can provide guidance and mentorship to team members as needed.

A strong pre-sales leader on a sales team should encourage continuous learning and development among the sales team members. Sometimes that means running tech training sessions for sales representatives to bring them up to speed on new technologies and concepts. That will also help foster a positive team culture focused on achieving sales goals, working collaboratively, and providing excellent customer service. Most importantly, it means you must lead by example through your actions and by producing positive results.

Leaders of Leaders

Regardless of the type of leadership, all three can lead leaders. A leader of leaders is someone who provides guidance to other leaders within an organization, all of whom have responsibilities for other own team members. These leaders have the ability to motivate and mentor other individuals, empowering them to step into leadership roles of their own.

They influence the organizational culture, empowering individuals across all levels to embrace more substantial roles and responsibilities. Leaders of leaders act as a coach and mentor, providing guidance and support to those they lead. They recognize and develop the potential in others by creating opportunities for them to grow and learn.

These leaders develop a sense of community within the organization where individuals from different groups work together to achieve common goals. They inspire and motivate others to achieve great things and create a culture of accountability and excellence within the organization.

Contrary to what you may think, this concept isn't exclusive to those in management roles. Even as an individual contributor, you can still serve as a leader of leaders. This is referred to as leading without influence.

Leading without influence means a person can lead and achieve a shared goal with a group without relying on formal authority or holding a position of power. Even while still being an individual contributor. They can achieve results and influence others through their personal qualities, skills, and actions. While demonstrating their expertise, building strong relationships, and communicating effectively to guide a team to a common goal. They inspire and motivate others through their activities. Through leading by example, they show the way rather than giving instructions. Leaders without influence build trust and respect among their peers, team members, and superiors and inspire and motivate others to join their causes.

All leaders, past and present, commonly exhibit a core set of leadership attributes. Some prime examples of these shared qualities include being a visionary, inspirational, decisive, adaptable, empathetic, and strategic. We can find many outstanding examples of these attributes in the past. Many famous leaders throughout history demonstrated unique leadership qualities that significantly impacted their respective fields. Here are some examples of influential leaders of the past putting these qualities into practice:

- **Visionary.** Martin Luther King Jr. and Henry Ford had a clear and compelling vision of the future they wanted to create, and they inspired others to work toward that vision. A visionary leader in pre-sales articulates a clear and compelling vision for how their company's products or services can help customers achieve their goals.
- **Inspirational.** Nelson Mandela and Steve Jobs inspired others to work toward a common goal through their words and actions. They communicated their message in a relatable and meaningful way to those around them. An inspirational pre-sales leader can motivate their team

to work toward a common goal by effectively communicating the value of their company's offerings.
- **Decisive.** Abraham Lincoln and Winston Churchill made tough decisions under pressure. A strong pre-sales leader can make quick decisions in the best interest of their team and the company, even in challenging situations.
- **Adaptable.** George Washington and Alexander the Great adapted to changing circumstances and led their troops to victory. An adaptable pre-sales leader can adjust their approach and strategies to meet the market's changing demands and the team's and customer's needs.
- **Empathetic.** Mahatma Gandhi and Mother Teresa understood and related to the needs and concerns of others. Put yourself in someone else's shoes to understand their specific needs.
- **Strategic.** Napoleon Bonaparte and Julius Caesar thought strategically and planned for the long-term success of their campaigns. A strategic pre-sales leader will always have a plan and is one step ahead of any challenges that may come their way. They plan for the worst but hope for the best.

Overall, some of the most outstanding leaders throughout history have demonstrated various leadership qualities we can apply in multiple situations and contexts. A pre-sales leader possessing these qualities can effectively lead their team, build strong relationships, and achieve the company's goals.

Regardless of the type of leader you are, there are many reasons you might want to move into a leadership role in pre-sales. Some reasons include the desire to have more responsibility, make more critical decisions, the opportunity to have a more significant impact on the company's success, the chance to earn a higher salary, gain more recognition, and the ability to improve your management skills. Many people find that being a leader can be rewarding, as it allows them to inspire and motivate others and help shape the organization's culture. Plus, it allows you to have a hand in influencing the future of your organization.

Chapter 8

The Future of Pre-Sales

Difficult to see. Always in motion is the future.

—Master Yoda

It's difficult to predict the exact future of pre-sales, as it depends on many factors. Factors such as market conditions, technological advancements, new expectations, and changing customer needs. However, the role of pre-sales will continue to evolve and become even more critical in the coming years. As companies increasingly rely on technology to drive their business operations, the demand for highly skilled pre-sales professionals who can help customers understand and implement complex technological solutions is likely to grow.

Additionally, the rise of new technologies—such as artificial intelligence, machine learning, and the Internet of Things—are likely to create new opportunities and challenges for pre-sales professionals. For example, pre-sales professionals may need to develop new skills and expertise to help customers understand and take advantage of these technologies. In the future, pre-sales professionals may also need to focus more on providing ongoing support and guidance to customers to help them get the most out of their technology solutions in the long term. It's possible that pre-sales professionals will focus more on providing business outcomes and less on product features.

I cannot stress the importance of continuous learning and development as crucial components for success in pre-sales as it allows you, as a solution architect, to stay current with the latest industry trends and technologies. It's also essential to learn about things outside your field of concentration to be more well-rounded, allowing you to see the bigger picture for your customers and enabling you to provide more value by supplying them with the best possible solutions for their business. It also helps you anticipate future trends and opportunities to be better prepared to address your customers' concerns and objections.

Continuous learning and development allow solutions architects to stay one step ahead of industry trends to stay relevant. Expanding your knowledge and skills will eventually benefit your career through future opportunities for advancement and growth.

It's not enough to only focus on improving your technical ability, you can't forget about improving your soft skills. Effective communication, negotiation, and leadership are vital for a solutions architect's success. By investing in continuous learning and development, you'll equip yourself with the tools you need to succeed and overcome future challenges. This preparation will also assist in career advancement as well.

Career Advancement Opportunities

Let's assume you've been a solutions architect for a few years and love what you do, but you want a change. The good news is there are many advanced career opportunities to consider. Each of the potential paths we'll discuss allows you to focus on the parts of the job you enjoy the most. One way to sort out these paths is to think of them in their areas of concentration. For example, some are product-focused, business-focused, technology-focused, or people-focused. Choosing your path depends on your interests and skills. That's one of the most exciting parts of working in pre-sales.

A product-focused solutions architect may be well-suited for a career in product management at some point. Assuming they're interested in understanding customer needs, market trends, and driving the product's future direction. They conduct market research, define the product vision, strategize, provide roadmaps, and collaborate with cross-functional teams. All to ensure the product is properly developed, launched on time, and meets the needs of the market it serves.

A business-focused solutions architect may want to consider a career as a field chief technology officer (field CTO), especially if they're interested in identifying a customer's business needs and focusing on big-picture outcomes. They understand the market, industry trends, competitive landscape, and identify new growth opportunities. They also drive the company's vision and strategy to provide specialized guidance throughout the sales process. Since field CTOs focus on the big picture, they rarely get caught up in the details. They focus more on creating business orientated outcomes, so they're less focused on the technology products that make those outcomes happen.

That brings us to the next path, a technology-focused principal solutions architect. These individuals enjoy thinking about the details, are very techy at heart, and are interested in providing their technical expertise to their customers. They work on unique scenarios that require large, complex solutions. Typically, these solutions are comprised of different technologies from many vendors. The projects they work on fundamentally change how customers use technology to run their businesses and how they view what technology can do for them going forward.

The last path is for those who are people focused. These individuals could enter a management role within their pre-sales organization. This path is for people passionate about providing guidance and mentoring others. They set goals and objectives, manage the team's workload, and facilitate collaboration within the organization. We reviewed some of these responsibilities in the previous section around leadership, but they're worth going over in more detail. This is an important role to any organization and is a popular path for many solutions architects.

In looking at what path may be best for you, it's important to consider where your passions lie. After thinking about these paths from a high level, which sounds the most interesting to you? Often your first feeling is the correct one, but let's take some time to look at these roles in more depth.

Product Management

Product management is a career advancement opportunity for pre-sales professionals with a strong understanding of the market and customer needs, along with the ability to work closely with cross-functional teams. Product managers not only manage the development and launch of new products or services. They also play a key role in driving the overall strategy and direction of the product.

The responsibilities of a product manager include:

- Conducting market research to understand customer needs and identify new opportunities.
- Defining the product vision, strategy, and roadmap.
- Collaborating with cross-functional teams, such as engineering, design, sales, and marketing, to ensure the product is developed and launched on time and within budget.
- Communicating with customers, stakeholders, and partners to ensure the product meets their needs and expectations.
- Monitoring and analyzing product performance and adjusting as needed.
- Keeping up to date with industry trends and the competitive landscape.

Product management roles often also require strong analytical and strategic thinking skills and the ability to communicate effectively with various stakeholders.

Pre-Sales professionals with experience working closely with customers and understanding their needs, as well as a deep understanding of the market and industry trends, can be well-suited for a career in product management. We should note that this is still a challenging role that requires a combination of technical, strategic, and leadership skills. However, it's an excellent opportunity for pre-sales professionals who want to impact the direction of the company's brand and its offerings.

Field CTO

The role of a field CTO in pre-sales is to act as a business advisor and subject matter expert for the sales team and their customers. The field CTO understands the business requirements to provide solutions to meet those requirements. This role often focuses on high-value, complex sales opportunities, where the business outcome for a customer is the key differentiator for the sales teams.

The field CTO is an evolution of a solutions architect, as the position typically requires higher levels of business expertise, a broader understanding of the market, and an awareness of upcoming industry trends. Sometimes field CTOs work closely with the product development team to ensure that future products align with the company's overall strategy and technical vision.

Field CTOs are a more advanced solutions architect and place more emphasis on the direction of a customer's business, product vision, and guidance for the sales team. They provide support throughout the sales process by working closely with the sales team to understand customers' business. This results in more defined requirements, allowing the sales team and their solutions architect to provide a wide range of technical solutions that create meaningful business outcomes.

Principal Solutions Architect

Now a principal solutions architect and a field CTO are both senior individual contributors within pre-sales that involve providing technical guidance and expertise. However, there are some critical differences between the two roles.

A principal solutions architect is typically a senior technical employee within an organization who focuses on the details. They go even deeper into the technological side of things and are some of the best subject matter experts in their field. They also play a crucial role in designing and developing some of the most advanced solutions proposed by their company.

Being a principal solutions architect can be a gratifying career for those with a passion for technology and a desire to dive deep into details. The ability to see the impact of your work, help other teams to achieve their goals, and the opportunity for continuous learning are some of the things that make this role rewarding. In this role, you'll work with cutting-edge technology and help shape your company's and its customers' technical strategy while having the chance to mentor and develop the technical aptitude of other solutions architects. Allowing them to grow and advance their technical aptitude.

Management

Finally, there's the management path for those who are more passionate about people than some of the other aspects of being a solutions architect. We touched on this previously when talking about being a leader of people. This career path is for folks who truly love being a mentor. They find it more rewarding seeing their mentee's success rather than their own personal achievements. This role is for those who'd rather be the coach on the sidelines instead of being the player on the field.

A good manager should realize they work for their team, not the other way around. Managers should understand that without their employees, there'd be no need for a manager. Therefore, it's crucial for managers to prioritize the needs of their team members and work collaboratively to achieve the organization's goals. They should take the time to understand the individual strengths and weaknesses of each team member and provide support, guidance, and resources to help them achieve their objectives. Managers should also be approachable and supportive, encouraging open communication and collaboration within the team.

The best way to think of this is to treat your team members like they're your customer. Just like how you would've done anything for your customers as a solutions architect, take that same approach with your team. This means following all the previous steps around effective communication and building trust, plus removing obstacles that prevent your team from achieving their objectives. If your team is successful, then you'll be successful.

When individual contributors feel valued and supported, they're more likely to be productive, engaged, and motivated to achieve their goals. This can lead to better performance, increased job satisfaction, and reduced turnover, resulting in a more successful and sustainable organization.

The specific responsibilities of a solutions architect manager may vary depending on the organization, but they typically include:

- **Setting goals and objectives for the team.** Management sets clear goals and objectives for the team and ensures they align with the organization's overall

strategy. That includes identifying areas for improvement and developing targets for the team.
- **Providing guidance and mentorship.** As a manager, you advise and mentor to help your team members develop their skills to be successful and ultimately aide in their future career advancement. This includes coaching and providing feedback on their performance and helping them identify areas for growth and improvement.
- **Managing your team's workload.** You manage the workload of the solutions architects to ensure they have the resources and support needed to be successful. This includes effectively allocating work to team members, providing help, and supporting them when needed. Your job is to prevent them from burning out while continuing to meet the needs of your organization.
- **Reviewing and approving proposed solutions and designs.** Sometimes you must review and support proposed solutions and designs to ensure they meet the organization's standards and requirements. That's especially important when you have newer members on your team.
- **Facilitating communication and collaboration.** You are the representative of your team and handle

collaboration between them and other groups within the organization. For example, sales, product development, installation services, and operations. This includes ensuring everyone knows the team's progress and priorities so they can work together effectively to achieve common goals.

Though a solutions architect manager leads and manages their team, there's a lot more they must do under the surface to help their team succeed. It's a critical role that involves managing the team's day-to-day activities, setting goals, providing mentorship, reviewing proposed solution designs, and facilitating collaboration between other organizations.

There are many advanced career paths in pre-sales you can take. It all depends on your skills, interests, and strengths. Each track offers different opportunities for growth and development. Think about what tasks you enjoy the most and get energy from. Do you find you are less tired when you spend your workday coaching other individuals or tinkering with technology? When you are doing something, you love it doesn't take as much out of you. This is a good indicator you may have a natural affinity to one path or another. It's essential as a solutions architect to understand your strengths and to pursue the route that aligns with your career goals.

Chapter 9

Final Thoughts

The way to get started is to quit talking and begin doing.

—Walt Disney

We've covered a lot in less than a hundred pages, but this book just scratches the surface of pre-sales. After all, depending on the products sold, the size of the company, and the industry, the role of pre-sales could change dramatically. The titles could be different, and they may not even call them solution architects, and that's okay. Though pre-sales may mean different things to different organizations, its overall purpose is still the same.

Pre-Sales identifies and develops potential sales opportunities before the formal sales process begins. It plays a crucial role in the process by working with customers to understand their needs and proposing solutions that meet them. To succeed you must have strong technical skills, effectively communicate, collaborate with cross-functional teams, understand their customer challenges, and have the expertise to solve those challenges. It's crucial to build trust and relationships with customers, understand sales, and handle objections.

The most important thing to being successful in pre-sales is having the ability to understand and respond to customers' pain points. Being able to build trust and relationships with customers by understanding the customer's business and objectives is an essential skill for pre-sales professionals.

It's essential to have a strong brand and to focus on continuous learning and development to advance your career. This goes hand in hand with handling objections and having sales acumen. Tailoring communication to your audience is another vital skill we touched on for building trust and understanding.

To infinity and...

In the future, pre-sales are expected to continue evolving with technology and the market. It will have a greater emphasis on digital and remote sales while still providing quality solutions tailored to the customer's specific needs. Solutions architects will need to stay up to date with the latest technologies, trends, and work well with others.

As society and business become more dependent on technology, the need for pre-sales within an organization will become increasingly important. As technology changes and becomes more complex, the need to understand how best to use it will grow. Pre-Sales professionals provide technical expertise to customers, helping them understand how a product or service can meet their needs and requirements.

With the speed at which technology is changing, it's impossible to predict what change tomorrow will bring. The best we can do is educate ourselves around emerging technology trends to keep up with what's coming down the road. Some technologies that may become more dependent on pre-sales professionals in the future include:

- **Artificial intelligence (AI) and machine learning (ML).** The investment in and development of AI and ML in recent years has been incredible. We're still years away from seeing its true potential, but it has already changed the way many companies work. Pre-Sales will be needed to help guide businesses to use AI effectively to stay competitive in their industry.

- **Cybersecurity.** Cybersecurity refers to the practice of protecting computer systems, networks, and sensitive information from theft, damage, or unauthorized access. The value of cybersecurity to a business lies in its ability to prevent financial loss, protect brand reputation, and maintain customer trust. Through the help of pre-sales, businesses will have better success implementing robust cybersecurity measures, reducing the risk of cyber-attacks, protecting their intellectual property, and ensuring compliance with industry regulations.
- **Cloud computing.** Multi-Cloud solutions are becoming increasingly popular among businesses that want to leverage the strengths of multiple cloud providers to meet their needs. As businesses move toward multi-cloud solutions, they'll need to develop cloud-native applications to run across multiple cloud platforms. Pre-Sales professionals can recommend the right cloud-native application development tools and help customers determine the right mix of cloud providers for their business needs.

- **Internet of Things (IoT).** The IoT refers to the interconnected network of physical devices, vehicles, buildings, and other objects embedded with sensors, software, and connectivity, allowing them to collect and exchange data. The value of the IoT to a business lies in its ability to optimize operations, reduce costs, and develop revenue streams by collecting and analyzing data from a variety of sources. Pre-Sales professionals can help businesses understand the value of the IoT then determine how they can integrate these IoT solutions into their existing environment.
- **Edge computing.** With the growth of 5G, there's a growing need for edge computing solutions that can process data closer to the source. Edge computing brings data processing and storage closer to the edge of the network. It enables businesses to process data in near real-time, which can lead to faster decision-making and increased operational efficiency. It can also reduce the risk of data breaches by keeping sensitive data closer to the source and providing greater control over data processing and storage.
- **Virtual reality (VR) and augmented reality (AR).** VR and AR are technologies that allow users to experience a simulated or enhanced version of reality. The value of

VR and AR to a business lies in their ability to enhance customer experiences, improve employee training, and create innovative marketing campaigns. Pre-Sales can help businesses understand the value of VR and AR and develop customized solutions that meet their unique requirements.

- **Blockchain.** Blockchain technology is becoming more prevalent in many industries. It enables secure and transparent transactions between parties without the need for intermediaries. The value of blockchain to a business lies in its ability to increase transparency, reduce costs, and improve security. It can be very complex, so pre-sales professionals can help businesses in their adoption of blockchain to streamline operations, reduce the risk of fraud, and provide greater visibility into their supply chains.

Overall, the role of pre-sales professionals will continue to be important in the future of technology as businesses seek to adopt new solutions and technologies to stay competitive and meet the changing needs of customers. The future of pre-sales is likely to be dynamic and exciting as the role continues to evolve and adapts to the marketplace's changing needs.

Call to Action

This book has taken you through the intricate world of pre-sales, from the introduction to potential futures to consider for your career. This is not an ending, but a call to action. Armed with newfound knowledge, you're poised to make a tangible impact. Let's talk about where you should start.

The first thing you should do is find yourself some mentors, as in plural. A mentor is a knowledgeable and experienced guide who offers support, advice, and insights to their mentee. Their value lies in providing direction, sharing wisdom, and facilitating growth, helping their mentee navigate challenges, make informed decisions, and reach their goals more effectively. So why would you want to limit yourself to only one mentor?

One of my own mentors once told me there are four types of mentors in the world: technical, career, leadership, and personal.

A technical mentor guides you in mastering specific skills, technologies, or expertise in your field. They offer insights, troubleshoot challenges, and provide guidance on technical matters, helping you enhance your proficiency.

A career mentor focuses on your professional growth and development. They offer advice on navigating your career path, making strategic decisions, setting goals, and seizing opportunities aligned with your aspirations.

A leadership mentor helps you cultivate leadership qualities and skills. They provide guidance on effective communication, decision-making, team management, and strategic thinking, empowering you to lead with confidence.

A personal mentor supports your overall personal development and well-being. They offer guidance on work-life balance, stress management, self-care, and building a positive mindset, helping you thrive both professionally and personally.

Just as a company's board of directors brings individuals with various expertise and insights together to guide its strategic decisions, your mentors serve as your personal board of directors. Each mentor contributes their unique knowledge and experience, representing different aspects of your growth. Having this "board" means you can tap into a rich pool of perspectives, advice, and guidance. Your board helps you make well-rounded decisions, navigate challenges, and seize opportunities with a broader understanding of both your strengths and areas for improvement. Just as a board enhances a company's success, your mentors enhance your personal and professional journey.

The second thing you should do is find yourself a mentee. Finding a mentee to give back to is vital because it establishes a reciprocal cycle of growth and success. By mentoring, you not only share your knowledge but also leave a lasting impact on your mentee's journey. This process benefits you through skill enhancement, fresh perspectives, networking, personal satisfaction, continuous learning, and contributing to industry growth. Mentoring is an investment that enriches both you and your mentee, fostering a sense of fulfillment and mutual achievement.

To be an effective mentor, focus on active listening, clear goal setting, and sharing your experiences and insights. Provide constructive feedback, guide critical thinking, and encourage problem-solving. Foster a supportive and open environment that values your mentee's growth and development, while also continuously learning and adapting your approach. Be open and honest about your experiences so your mentee can learn from your mistakes and hopefully avoid them. A good mentor is someone who lifts their mentee up so they can reach higher and be more successful than their mentor ever was.

The third thing is to go learn something new. Find a certification to get, a new book to read, or a professional challenge to conquer. As I've mentioned many times, we must keep learning. We're both teachers and students. It can be argued that in pre-sales our competitiveness and drive to win align with the spirit of an athlete. Just as professional athletes dedicate themselves to daily training for their games, we too should engage in ongoing self-improvement. Find new things to keep yourself sharp.

Find a goal that scares you. Then challenge yourself to achieve that goal. It will take time, and you may not be successful at first, but you'll learn so much every step of the way. Then, eventually, you'll find success. For me, it was writing this book.

I'm dyslexic and spent a lot of my early academic life in tutoring and trying to catch up to my peers. I never gave up, and I attacked the problem head on. After joining the workforce, I started a technical blog where I shared what I learned with a broader audience. My blog allowed me to work through my learning disability to stay sharp. Eventually, my wife inspired me to take my writing to the next level and self-publish my book, and here we are.

The point is that facing and embracing challenges that initially seem intimidating or even frightening can lead to growth, valuable learning experiences, and eventual success. I want to emphasize the importance of setting ambitious goals that push you beyond your comfort zone, even if it means dealing with obstacles or setbacks along the way. By pursuing such goals, you can acquire new skills, knowledge, and resilience. With a willingness to confront fears, you can achieve significant accomplishments that may have once seemed impossible, such as writing and self-publishing a book in the face of a learning disability.

About the Author

Nathaniel Fagundo has had a diverse array of roles within the IT field throughout his career, with a substantial portion of his expertise spanning over a decade in pre-sales. During this period, he diligently worked his way up the ranks, and eventually became one of the top 1% of solutions architects at a top-Fortune 500 technology company. His dedication is underscored by the accumulation of nearly forty distinct technical certifications, the creation of specialized training programs for his pre-sales community, and the establishment of his own blog.

In addition to his professional accomplishments, Nathaniel has actively engaged with prominent organizations, including being part of VMware's vExperts and Dell's CTO Ambassadors team. He has also contributed his time and expertise to volunteer efforts, working with organizations like "Minority Wealth Gap" and "Girls Who Game" Both sharing a goal of addressing the needs of underserved communities by promoting equity and opportunity.

During his tenure in pre-sales, Nathaniel has functioned as a reliable consultant to numerous clients spanning various industries, including local government, healthcare, financial services, retail, higher education, and select nonprofit sectors, assisting them in integrating new technology to facilitate business transformations.

Most importantly, he is a proud husband to his wife and college sweetheart, Urmila.

Printed in Great Britain
by Amazon